WEDDING FLOWERS

WEDDING FLOWERS

PAULINE MANN

Photographs by Derick Bonsall
Drawings by Wendy Goodwill

B.T. Batsford Ltd   London

Frontispiece: *Warm autumn colouring for the autumn bride. Gladioli, dahlias, cream carnations and longiflorum lilies were arranged with berried* cotoneaster, Thalictrum adiantifolium *and* Rosa rubrifolia *in a small window alcove. St Everilda's, Nether Poppleton, York.* (Arranger: Pauline Mann.)

For Claudia, Elisabeth and Philip

ISBN 0 7134 4636 6

Typeset by Tek-Art Ltd, Kent
Printed in Hong Kong
for the publishers
B.T. Batsford Ltd
4 Fitzhardinge Street
London W1H 0AH

ACKNOWLEDGMENT

My warmest thanks to Wendy Goodwill N.D.D., D.A.(Manc), A.T.D., Lecturer in Art, York College of Arts and Technology, for doing the line drawings, and to Derick Bonsall, ARPS, for taking all the photographs.

I would also like to thank the following people:

The clergy who have been so co-operative and patient and have allowed me to arrange flowers and have them photographed: The Rt Rev. Ronald Jasper, former Dean of York; Canon Jack Armstrong, Rector of All Saints, Pavement, York; The Rev. Alan Heslop, Vicar of St Olave's, Marygate, York; The Rev. Jeremy Howat, Vicar of St Giles, Skelton, York; The Rev. Arthur West, Vicar of All Saints, Upper Poppleton and St Everilda's, Nether Poppleton; The Rev. Richard Noyes, Vicar of St Andrew's, Aldborough, Boroughbridge.

Captain V.M. Wombwell for permitting photography in Newborough Priory; Christine Schofield for styling the hair and Irene Bough for making the headdresses and bouquets; the brides who so kindly let their wedding flowers be used for this book; finally, the many flower arranging friends who have helped me.

CONTENTS

INTRODUCTION: PLANNING THE FLOWERS

This book is concerned with the sociable wedding, whether it is to be an especially big occasion with hundreds of guests, or a quiet little gathering of close friends and family. I have assumed trouble will be taken to make the event a visual delight.

Flowers take one of the leading roles at weddings. There may or may not be quantities of expensive blooms, but whatever arrangements are envisaged, these need to be planned. The flower arrangements must be in keeping with the surroundings and in harmony with the general colour scheme, and they must be properly placed so that they are seen to the best advantage by as many people as possible. Three really striking displays are bettter than four times that number of insignificant arrangements, and quite inexpensive flowers can be very effective.

MAKING A BEGINNING

When the date for the wedding is fixed and the church chosen (usually the bride's parish church), she and her mother (or whoever will play the part of hostess) can begin to think of the decorations. Permission must always be sought from the incumbent of the parish to allow special arrangements, so get the permission early, just in case certain things are not welcome. There is no point in planning what you cannot have. Some churches do not have flowers on the altar, and many clergy have strict rules about flowers during Lent and Advent. These are penitential seasons and, by ancient tradition, not the time for a wedding. If a wedding is to take place at such a season then you may be required to remove the flowers so they will not be in the church for the following Sunday. There will be a member of the congregation in charge of the flower rota and the incumbent will put you in touch with her. She will notify the person whose turn it will be to do the flowers the Sunday after your wedding – an important piece of diplomacy.

Most churches are architecturally interesting and will have certain unique features. Don't obscure these, but try, if possible, to emphasize them. Aim to put the decorations above eye level whenever practicable so that they are not lost to sight when people stand up.

The correct colour for frontals and vestments at a wedding is white. It would be wise to confirm that this will be so. By no means all churches possess white altar frontals.

Note also the colour of the carpet in the sanctuary, for that cannot be changed.

Make sure you have considered the following:

✳ Does the church own some pedestals or other containers that you can use, and do the pillars have any screws or nails for hanging garlands?

✳ Will the pews take pew-ends easily?

✳ Is the church normally kept locked, and if so who has the keys?

✳ Are there weekday services that would preclude flowers being arranged at those times? Town churches usually have many weekday services.

✳ Where is the water? Where are the

An example of flowers well matched to the altar frontal – one of the factors that must be taken into account in any church. The bride wanted white and cream and as it was early November there were plenty of small chrysanthemums available. The dainty hybrid lily 'Juliana' added a touch of luxury and a change of form. The foliage was golden yew, Viburnum tinus, *box and trails of ivy and periwinkle, both variegated. In winter evergreen foliage can be rather sombre unless some variegated material is included.*

The mechanics on each side consisted of a whole block of foam in a shallow, elliptical black plastic dish capped with wire netting. The ledge was narrow and precluded the insertion of very much plant material into the back of the arrangements for ballast, so some stones were put into the containers, behind the foam, to eliminate the risk of their toppling forwards. Special tape, made to stretch across the foam and fastening it to the container, can often be used instead of wire netting, but the netting does help to take the weight of strong, thick stems, so making safer mechanics. All Saints, Pavement, York. (Arranger: Pauline Mann.)

dustpans and brushes? Where does the rubbish go?

✳ How will you go about dismantling and recovering any pedestals of your own?

All this information can then be passed on to whoever is to do the flowers, although the arrangers will certainly wish to see the church for themselves.

WHO WILL DO THE FLOWERS?

A professional firm will naturally comply with the bride's requests and the job should be efficiently done; but it will be expensive, for you will be paying for labour as well as for the flowers. There are the semi-professionals who will estimate the cost of the flowers and foliage and charge a modest fee for their work. But usually flower arranging friends of the family love to be asked to carry out the decorating for nothing more than their expenses, and, one hopes, a present! Many hours of thought and hard work go into every arrangement: choosing and cutting the foliage, ordering and collecting the flowers, finding the right containers, conditioning the plant material overnight, assembling the mechanics and transporting everything to the church. All this has to be done before a single bloom is put in place. But the arrangers will enjoy every minute of their task.

7

ONE

THE ALTAR AND CHANCEL

There are four places for altar flowers: on the altar, on a ledge behind it (if there is one), in pedestals on either side and on the altar steps. This last position is most effective where there are several steps leading to a raised altar.

During the last decade many altars have been moved from the east end of the church to a central place in the chancel, or sometimes into the nave, much nearer to the congregation. One of the results has been the banishment of the traditional pair of matching brass vases that stood either side of the cross. As the officiating clergyman stands behind the altar facing his flock, vases of flowers would be a hazard, and pedestals are used instead. But if a bride particularly wants flowers on the altar these might be permitted, and a low arrangement on one side gives a pleasing asymmetrical effect which is far less formal than a similar pair, and more suitable for a modern church.

However, there are still plenty of churches where the altar remains at the east end, though the trumpet-shaped vases are nearly always things of the past. If you do have to use them it is possible to fix a large candle-cup or plastic foam saucer to the top. This makes the arranging easier, for you can use foam and the result will be softer and prettier. There was something rather endearing about those well-polished brass vases!

Sometimes an altar has a reredos with a ledge below it. This is a good place for flowers, for they can spread the whole length of the ledge if you wish.

Pedestals, either on one or both sides of the altar, make splendid focal points. They should be large enough to be commanding and they will carry the eye to the east end of the church.

Flowers arranged on the altar steps look beautiful but their effectiveness depends upon there being a good difference in height between the nave and the altar.

The entrance to the chancel is another key position and tall arrangements either side will be enjoyed by everyone. As the couple take their vows at this spot the flowers are totally part of the scene. But remember, some arrangement at the east end is needed, otherwise the eye stops at the chancel flowers instead of moving on to the altar.

A screen between the nave and chancel gives the opportunity to make an archway there. Usually this is done by using matching pedestals either side of the entrance to the chancel and fixing flowers, in foam, to the arch of the screen. This looks most spectacular but is not always possible because the incumbent may be reluctant to allow the necessary mechanics to be attached to the screen's woodwork. If allowed, it does have to be done with the greatest care, and is most rewarding.

You may feel tempted to decorate the front of the choir stalls, especially when they are of solid wood. This is a place where garlands look particularly well. If you decide to have garlands, make quite sure they can be attached without hurting the woodwork. It is often quite simple to use the stems of lamps or candle-holders and suspend garlands from these with fine wire. (For instructions for making a garland, see

Longiflorum lilies arranged so that each flower can be clearly seen placed on one side of an altar. They are in a modern black metal container that matches the cross and candlesticks. Some trails of canariensis ivy hang down over the front of the altar. All Saints, Upper Poppleton, York. (Arranger: Mollie Howgate.)

The ironwork of the pedestal has a modern look which fits in with the altar furnishings. The flowers were arranged fairly traditionally except that the shape was not too rigidly triangular.

Not much foliage was used apart from some arching sprays of cotoneaster, some curving prunus branches and flowing lengths of periwinkle, all necessary to counteract the straight stems of the larkspur which gave a spiky outline. There were also pale pink carnations, some clusters of the old 'American Pillar' rose recessed for depth of colour, a few long-stemmed lilac sweet peas, erigeron and large, strong stems of Lilium speciosum 'Rubrum'. The pedestal matched the windows described on page 26 (top).

Note: I have mentioned the risk of discoloration from lily pollen in the plant list. L. speciosum 'Rubrum' has particularly dark and prolific pollen! Although it is sad to mutilate flowers, it is only sensible to cut off the swinging hinged anthers from the end of the filaments, otherwise clothes can be ruined and the flower's own petals stained and spoilt. All Saints, Upper Poppleton, York. (Arranger: Pauline Mann.)

One of a matching pair of arrangements on the steps leading to the high altar in York Minster. As the season was late autumn maximum use was made of chrysanthemums – large white reflex blooms, anemone-flowered and cream spider varieties. There were also cream carnations and longiflorum lilies. The foliage included sweeping curved branches of Cotoneaster 'Cornubius', laurel, large bergenia leaves and Hedera canariensis 'Variegata'. These arrangements at each side of the altar both needed a black-painted tin 26 × 26 cm (10 × 10 in.) into which two blocks of soaked foam were placed, leaving enough room for two 10 cm (4 in.) pin-holders in the back of the tin for ballast; this was important, as the flow of the flowers was downwards. Stones would have done as a substitute for the pin-holders. The foam was also capped with 5 cm (2 in.) chicken wire, secured to the tins with reel wire. York Minster. (Arranger: Janet Hayton.)

Early autumn is an especially good time for garland making. This is because there are so many seed heads, fruits and berries to gather. The photograph shows a garland designed to hang on the front of the vicar's stall and it measured about 0.9 metres (3 feet). The foliage was Viburnum tinus, an ivy with a cream variegation (Hedera helix 'Harald'), and Chamaecyparis 'Plumosa', a feathery tree. The fruits were those of the Rosa rugosa 'Frau Dagmar Hastrup'; the flowers were from the hybrid tea rose 'Guenevere', and pink spray carnations.

The usual mechanics of foam 'sausages' covered with wire netting were used. The ends of the stall projected upwards so that reel wire fixed to the wire netting held the garland in position. St Everilda's, Nether Poppleton, York. (Arranger: Pauline Mann.)

pages 17–18.) Tall flowers can be put in low containers on the floor in front of the choir stalls as an alternative to garlands, but unless the chancel is several steps higher than the nave these arrangements may be lost to view when the congregation stands up.

TWO

TALL FREE-STANDING ARRANGEMENTS

The height of this arrangement is around 3 metres (10 feet). It was designed as one of a matching pair for a large building. The stand was made from a 2 metre (6 feet), 5 × 5 cm (2 × 2 in.) stake of wood fixed with angle brackets to a base. The base was two squares of 2.5 cm (1 in.) chip board, one 35 cm (14 in.) and the other 30.5 cm (12 in.). The stake has four platforms for containers, each measuring 12.7 × 17.75 cm (5 × 7 in.). The top platform is screwed and glued onto the top of the stake; the others were fixed by angle brackets under the platforms. The whole was painted a neutral grey.

In order to get the necessary height, the two top platforms were arranged first and then the whole stand was lifted on to a plinth 1 metre (3 feet) tall. The stand was wired to the plinth and the boat-shaped plastic containers had their foam covered with wire netting. Reel wire threaded through the wire netting fixed the containers to the stand. The season was winter and the flowers were cream and white chrysanthemums, cream carnations and some 'Destiny' lilies. The foliage was evergreen, but plenty of variegated ivy introduced colour. York Minster. (Arranger: Pauline Mann.)

PEDESTALS

NAFAS has done a great deal to improve the standard of flower arrangement throughout Britain. This is very noticeable in churches, most of which now have at least one pedestal; these are nearly always made of black or white painted wrought iron with some sort of integral container (which should be shallow) and the best are telescopic.

All tall free-standing arrangements can be placed where you wish: on both sides or one side of the altar or at the chancel steps. Standing in the porch or at the back of the church, they give a welcome to the guests. Pedestals are not the prerogative of churches and can perfectly well be used in the home or any other place as long as there is room enough to be able to stand back and appreciate them. They also look much better with a plain background.

COLUMNS

The wooden column on a plinth, with a flat platform on top for the container, is a variation of the pedestal. Columns look very dignified and are suited to many churches. They also are attractive in the home.

TORCHÈRES

The torchère, the coveted polished wood eighteenth-century light stand, so much in demand today for raised arrangements, is a piece of domestic furniture. Beautiful for pedestal-type designs in the home, it can look somewhat out of place in other environments.

THE ZIG-ZAG

The zig-zag is a modern way of presenting a mass of flowers. Zig-zags are made from a central wooden or iron support fixed to a heavy base – the heavy base is most important. There is a top platform and lower platforms alternating from side to side down the stem, not too close together. There is a description of a wooden zig-zag in the caption on page 13. When made of iron the platforms have to be welded on.

SHAPE

There is no reason why tall and impressive designs on columns and pedestals should be triangular in outline. Loose circles and ovals of flowers are lovely and the Dutch-Flemish flower paintings of the seventeenth and eighteenth centuries on which our present-day traditional arrangements are based often had flat tops and were irregular in outline.

MECHANICS FOR LARGE ARRANGEMENTS

Strong mechanics are essential for every arrangement but they are especially important for heavy masses of flowers.

Plastic foam

There are many makes of plastic foam. The blocks need to be soaked in water for approximately ten minutes, or until they sink to the bottom of the basin, but certainly not for hours. When used correctly, foam makes flower arranging easier and quicker and gives a gentle flowing line. There are certain points to remember:

✳ Always have the foam for a large arrangement not less than 7.5 cm (3 in.) above the rim of the container.

✳ Do not fill a container with foam; leave a space around the block. If the foam touches the rim it makes watering extremely difficult and you risk the plant material, particularly hairy leaves, gathering up the water and syphoning it on to the floor.

✳ As foam is lightweight some kind of ballast is often necessary, especially on ledges where there is no room for plant material to be put into the back of an arrangement to balance it. Pin-holders, special foam-holders and stones help to stabilize flowers in these positions.

✳ It is safer, with a free-standing design, to secure the container to the column or stand, thus avoiding any risk of disaster should it be moved or knocked. Wire netting and/or a

The large raised arrangement was for a wedding at the beginning of February. It was placed on a wooden column instead of being arranged in the more familiar wrought-iron pedestal. Some of the forsythia was cut from the garden and brought into the gentle heat of the house three weeks before the wedding, but the shops also had splendid branches of this lovely early shrub. The forsythia, Garrya elliptica with its grey catkins, some hazel catkins, Salix glandulosa 'Setsuka' and a few pieces of western hemlock were used for height and spread. Too much evergreen material was avoided as it can appear heavy and reminiscent of Christmas, and spoil the open feeling given by burgeoning spring branches. The white iris had long stems. The tulips were strengthened by having most of their leaves removed before being wrapped in newspaper and conditioned for 36 hours; this treatment made them develop well. Only a couple of tubes were needed to raise a few flowers. The mimosa softened and filled what would have otherwise been rather a 'stemmy' group.

This large arrangement consisted of 12 stems of forsythia of various lengths, three bunches of long-stemmed white irises, three packs of mimosa, four bunches of yellow daffodils and about 15 tulips, some yellow and some white.

The mechanics were the usual wire netting-topped foam in a large shallow tin. This was secured to the column with reel wire to avoid any risk of the container moving on its stand. St Olave's, Marygate, York. (Arranger: Mollie Sykes.)

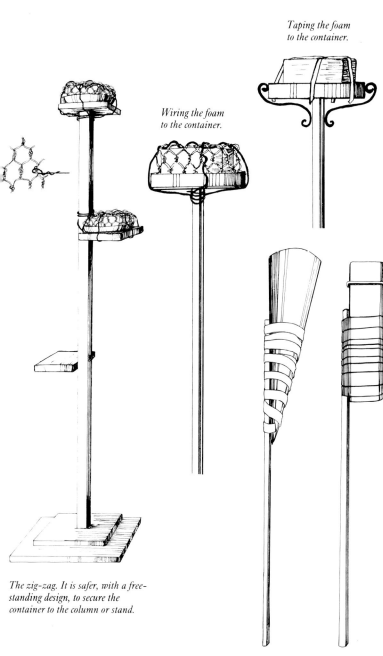

Taping the foam to the container.

Wiring the foam to the container.

The zig-zag. It is safer, with a free-standing design, to secure the container to the column or stand.

Cones and tubes.

specially manufactured tape which straps the foam to the container will both do this job, but the wire netting also strengthens the mechanics by helping to take the weight of long, heavy, thick-stemmed plant material when it is placed in the foam.

Everything that contributes to the total stability of an arrangement should be used.

Wire netting for garlands and swags

Wire netting is pliable and although it bends it also holds any shape you require. Plastic foam wrapped in thin polythene is too slippery and uncontrollable, but encased in wire netting it will stay exactly as you want it. Sphagnum moss can be a substitute for plastic foam for garlands, swags and cones.

Wire netting and pin-holder in a deep container

Before the days of plastic foam, crumpled 5 cm (2 in.) mesh wire netting made good mechanics in a deep container. Its use is improved if a large pin-holder is first put into the bottom of the container and fixed there with one of the materials specially made for this purpose. The wire netting is loosely crumpled and placed over the pin-holder. This gives a stable place for anchoring the main stems and subsidiary stems can be held by the wire netting. This method ensures a plentiful supply of water.

Cones or tubes

Plastic cones and tubes, wired or taped onto thin, green-painted canes, may be needed in order to lift some short-stemmed flowers higher in the arrangement, but keep these to a minimum for they have to be hidden. Choose long-stemmed flowers whenever possible and tall pieces of foliage. Height brings the arrangement above eye level and gives elegance. The scale of the flowers is important and bold forms are needed.

AMOUNTS AND COSTS

There are so many variable factors to be

15

reckoned with that it is not easy to estimate the amount of flowers for the average pedestal. I have quoted the numbers of flowers and quantities of foliage used in some of the captions to the photographs.

In winter, foliage has to be evergreen, and this can be bulky and visually heavy, whereas a spring pedestal using flowering shrubs which have not yet produced leaves will look sparse and lightweight and need more actual blooms than a winter one.

Zig-zags, because of the platforms at different levels all holding containers, present the flowers at several heights and will not need such long-stemmed material as the columns and pedestals. They are, therefore, economical, for they make a good show with simpler material. They are particularly useful for short-stemmed spring flowers.

The aim for all free-standing arrangements is to get a three-dimensional look. Sometimes an arrangement is actually seen from all round, but even if it is viewed only from the front, do give the illusion of all-roundness by taking the foliage to the back and placing flowers low down into the back of the design. These blooms will carry the eye through the arrangement and give the necessary feeling of depth.

THREE

PILLARS, WINDOWS AND PEW-ENDS

A graceful torchère used as a stand for flowers at a wedding reception. In the arrangement were a mixture of July garden flowers and a few blooms from the florist. From the garden were larkspur, Ester Reads, Achillea 'The Pearl', mallow, pink pyrethrums and pink and white roses; from the florist longiflorum lilies, 'Bonny Jean' spray chrysanthemums, both spray and large carnations and gypsophila. The large drawing-room, Newborough Priory, Coxwold, Yorkshire. (Arranger: Eileen Gaskell.)

PILLAR DECORATIONS

Flowers on pillars are high enough to be enjoyed by everyone, whether sitting or standing. Garlands are evocative of celebrations throughout the ages, and in Renaissance Italy the young men would stretch beribboned garlands of fresh flowers across the street for a wedding.

Because of this romantic association it would be lovely to think of twining garlands around columns in church. Unfortunately, unless the pillars are not very high this would be an extremely lengthy task, needing metres of garland. A less demanding treatment would be to garland the pillars once only, just below the capital. This is effective and not too time-consuming.

Gothic piers

These are far too massive even to think of encircling; instead a swag, or a long garland, can be hung vertically in one of the recesses.

Fresh garlands are best made out of sections of soaked foam, and a 22.85 cm (9 in.) block, cut vertically into four lengths, will make a garland over a metre long. Wrap the four lengths of foam in a continuous piece of polythene or clinging film, leaving 5 cm (2 in.) between the sections and wiring these spaces. Each section of foam needs its own compartment and a little space to spare, otherwise you will be unable to curve the garland; also, by wiring between the sections you stop the water running from the top to the bottom – should the garland be hung

vertically. At this stage you will have mechanics that resemble a string of green sausages.

Next cut a 20.3 cm (8 in.) width of 2.5 cm (1 in.) mesh wire netting, long enough to enfold the 'sausages', leaving a short length to spare at either end which might be useful for hanging purposes. Fasten the netting carefully around the wrapped foam and try not to puncture the polythene. Use the joined netting side as the front; you will then have a smooth back to the garland which will not scratch the surface onto which it is hung. Obviously more sections of foam would be needed for a longer garland and fewer or shorter pieces for a shorter one. These mechanics are absolutely firm yet remain easy to bend if you should want a looped garland. When curved, the wire netting will hold its shape perfectly.

There must be a hook, nail or screw to take the decoration, and once one is carefully put into position by someone who knows what should be done, it will remain for future occasions and is a valuable asset. Even a garland as long as 3.5 metres (12 feet) will hang successfully, with no extra support, as long as it is encased in wire netting. Anything longer than this needs to be backed by a wooden batten about 5 cm (2 in.) wide and 2.5 cm (1 in.) deep. Nails or screws put in at regular intervals down the length of the batten will hook onto the netting at the back of the garland, supporting it and keeping it straight. The batten will require a hook at the top, for in this case it is the batten and not the wire netting which is the means of hanging. Two holes, drilled through the top end of the batten and threaded with stout wire, may be more satisfactory than a hook; it depends upon the type of screw or nail on which it has to be hung. The garland should be put into position on the wood and hooked to it before it is hoisted up. Do this job on the floor.

Another way of making a garland
This method will give a slightly different effect.

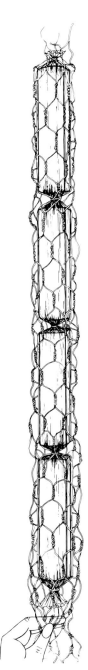

Fasten the netting carefully around the wrapped foam 'sausages'.

Very long garlands need to be backed by a wooden batten, with nails or screws put in down the length of it to hook on to the wire netting.

18

Plastic cones may be taped to a batten at regular intervals.

Singly wired bows and tails are best.

The finished garland must hang straight. Plastic cones may be taped to a batten at regular intervals; they should be close enough together to give a garland-like appearance when the cones are filled with flowers and foliage. Soaked foam is first fitted into the cones, projecting well above each cone's rim in order to get plenty of downward flow. This method takes rather more and rather longer pieces of plant material, but some arrangers find it easier to do. My own opinion is that 'sausages' in wire netting are very straightforward to cope with and also give a more graceful effect.

CHURCH WINDOWS

Window ledges are stages for flowers for they have the advantage of being at eye level or above it. They often get rather pedestrian treatment, with the flowers placed centrally, so that in the daytime tall flowers disappear with the light behind them. Decorations on flat window ledges are a simple way of making a church look special, and do not take too many flowers.

Windows with a wide sill

When there is a wide sill the flowers may be arranged on either side, making the window's embrasure a background for the tallest plant material with the rest of it flowing towards the centre of the sill at a much lower height. In this way the flowers are not seen against the light quite so much. The two sides do not need symmetrical treatment; it is more attractive when one side is of lesser importance, and the important sides can alternate in adjacent windows. Always allow some trailing pieces of foliage to escape over the straight sill edge to give a softening effect.

Sloping sills

Sloping sills can be a problem. Church congregations who take their decorating seriously often have platforms made (see photograph on page 27 [bottom]). It is still necessary to keep the flowers arranged on these platforms low, but an inverted crescent shape is pretty, and for this you will need plenty of curving plant material. The mechanics must be plastic foam in a shallow container. This will be hidden by the foliage and flowers.

Colourful stained glass windows

Very colourful glass is a challenge and I am not sure that it shouldn't be left in its glory. If you feel you want to decorate a brilliant window choose one or at the most, two of the colours in the glass and use tints and tones of this, or these. Never try to match every hue.

Garlanded windows

Garlands always look festive and although they take a little time to make they can be done well in advance and have the flowers added at the last moment the day before the wedding. When they are to be used for windows their length depends on the windows' width and the depth of curve required. It is as well to see whether there are some handy screws or nails for the garlands to hang on before you decide to have them. There are often some projections at the base of the windows, just below the glass, onto which thin wires can be fixed. Another method is to paint thin dowelling rods an inconspicuous colour and wedge these tightly across the bottom of the windows. They can then be used for wires or ribbons. Another idea is to have arrangements either side of the window sills which will camouflage weights to which the garlands may be attached.

Flat, low window sills

Just occasionally the window ledges are below eye level and these look very striking if they are treated like window boxes. The mechanics for these are blocks of foam in shallow oblong containers. Keep the flowers and plants low and entirely fill the space.

PEW-ENDS

I thoroughly recommend pew-end decorations.

They transform the nave into a floral avenue which is exactly what is wanted for the progress of the bridal party up and down the aisle. There is no need to have flowers on every pew-end; they can be hung at the end of alternate rows or even on every third or fourth row when the aisle is a long one. As for all topiary trees, garlands and swags, the foliage may be put into the mechanics in advance – the day before the wedding or sooner than that – and the flowers added at the last minute. Do remember that all polythene or clinging film-wrapped blocks of foam will drip for a short time when they are first hung, so be prepared for this to happen. It will soon stop, and making up the decorations a while before the wedding helps to solve this minor problem. Bows of ribbon (wire a single loop at a time) may be mixed amongst the flowers, and when the pew-ends have stopped dripping they can be given tails of ribbon.

Very simple and effective pew-ends can be made on lengths of thin wood with holes drilled through them. I have often made two hooks of 18 gauge wire, taped them to eliminate any risk of their scratching the pew's surface and bent them to fit the curve of the pew.

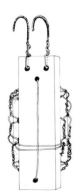

Mechanics

Very simple and effective pew-ends can be made on lengths of thin wood or peg-board approximately 5-7 cm (2-3 in.) wide. The length depends on the desired finished shape and size of the decoration. Solid pieces of wood must have holes drilled through them (see diagram on page 20), but peg-board has holes already made. The pieces of wood in the illustration are about 15.25 cm (6 in.) long and were painted a matt dark green, using an undercoat. Blocks of foam 10 cm (4 in.) long by 5 cm (2 in.) deep and 8 cm (3 in.) wide were wrapped in thin polythene before being placed on the boards where they were held in position with small pieces of wire netting anchored to the wood by lengths of reel wire threaded through the holes.

Hanging pew-ends

Some pews have 'swan-necked' ends around which cord, ribbon or wire will go easily and hang straight. Cord or ribbon can be obtrusive and detract from the flowers unless it hangs vertically; it looks ungainly stretched around a fat pew-end! Ends of pews that are on the same level as the backs of the pews are not the easiest for mechanics. It is most unlikely you will find a screw or nail onto which you will be able to fix the decorations, and the method chosen to hang them depends very much on their weight. I have great faith in the two-sided sticky pads or sticky rolls which are obtainable at a hardware store or stationer. Each single pad is said to be able to bear 0.25 kg (8 oz) of weight, so four to six of these – or the equivalent cut from a roll and stuck onto the back of the 15.25 cm (6 in.) lengths of wood – will hold most modestly sized pew-ends. The back of the wood must be absolutely smooth and dry, then they will stick like limpets and leave no marks at all when removed.

The same lengths of wood, of a width of 5-7 cm (2-3 in.), can be stuck with double-sided pads to the flat vertical tops of pew-ends when these have a width of 3.7 cm (1½ in.) or so. The same mechanics of foam, wire and polythene should be used. This way of arranging the flowers will give a different but equally attractive result, with plant material upright but trailing down on the aisle side.

Another possibility for difficult-to-fix pew-ends is to use fishing line, for this is both strong and almost invisible. Threaded through the holes drilled in the wooden backing it will go over the ends of the pews and can be fastened with dark sticky tape. Again, avoid too much weight.

I have often made two hooks of 18-gauge wire by passing it through the holes at the top of the wood and then taping these to eliminate any risk of their scratching the pew's surface. Then they are bent to fit the curve of the pew. This works very efficiently.

It is possible to buy plastic foam-holders with handles that will hang on a hook or nail. They are rather large, however, and take a lot of plant material. I also always prefer to have the extra strength given by the pieces of wire netting and this can only be achieved by using the wood or peg-board, for the netting must be fixed with reel wire through the holes in the backing boards.

FOUR

THE ENTRANCE

THE CHURCH PORCH

A porch may be large enough for a pedestal or similar raised arrangement, but failing this there are sometimes window recesses that will take flowers, or a bench on one or both sides that could be used. In any entrance-way the decorations need to be out of the way of passers-by or they will get knocked and spoilt. When space is restricted a hanging ball or wire basket could be the answer, for anything suspended is conveniently safe from buffeting. Make sure, as always, that there is something from which to hang the ball or basket before you embark on this means of decoration.

Hanging balls
These are very simple to make using the same mechanics as you would for a swag or garland. Prepare a 15.25 cm (6 in.) cube of polythene-covered foam enclosed in wire netting. The cord or ribbon for hanging will slot through the top of the wire netting: check for length. If you add ribbon tails, let the arrangement finish dripping before fixing them. Singly wired bows and tails are best.

Hanging baskets
A wire basket of the kind used in summer to hang above the doorway makes a perfect decoration. It must hang straight – nothing looks worse than one of these suspended out of the vertical. It can be lined with sphagnum moss and planted with rooted plants, or be given a block of polythene-covered wet foam and treated as a container for cut flowers; in the latter case the plant material is placed in the underside as well as the sides. It will drip for an hour or so, so allow for this to happen. A woven plant material basket does not look quite right as a raised container: however much flow you try to give it there is no escaping the fact that the underside was made to stand on a solid surface and not to be viewed from below! So, if you want baskets of flowers, hang them at eye level or below.

THE FONT

Fonts are usually situated near to the main entrance. This is a symbolic position, signifying the first step along the Christian road of life, baptism. But at a christening there is not room for flowers too near the font, neither can the top be used as a raised column as it is so often for a flower festival, harvest festival and other important occasions. A flowery font makes a welcoming display for guests entering the church. Try not to obscure it if it is architecturally interesting.

ARCHWAYS

An archway of flowers sounds very lavish, but it need not be expensive if simple flowers are used and the church has the mechanics in stock. Many churches use a decorated archway for festivals during the year, particularly on Palm Sunday, when it is called a Jerusalem archway and spans the outer door of a church. The name commemorates Christ's entry into Jerusalem on Palm Sunday. However, the idea may be used

One of a matching pair of garlands. The foliage was mostly cupressus and the flowers were those obtainable all the year round: spray carnations, spray chrysanthemums and single blooms of 'Prospect' lilies. St Andrew's, Aldborough, Boroughbridge. (Arrangers: Jean Lock and Patricia Hesford.)

for any special occasion. You will need a foundation of trellis framework fixed to the porch. Blocks of clinging film or polythene-wrapped foam (whether you strengthen these further with wire netting depends on the type of trellis) are fastened to the frame with reel wire and used for the stems of foliage, making a background for as many flowers as you want and can afford. It looks good even when only foliage is used. This makes an impressive frame for the photographs taken at the church doorway.

TOPIARY TREES

This is another way of embellishing the entrance, either at the church or the reception. So often it is these small touches, which are slightly out of the usual mode of decorating, that add distinction to an occasion. Many flower clubs have the containers already set up and will either lend or hire them for a small fee. These containers are most likely to be plastic copies of classical shapes, painted to simulate stone or bronze. The poles will be set in concrete and for the best results should have two holes drilled through them, one approximately 2.5 cm (1 in.) from the top, and the other 28 cm (11 in.) below the first. This gap will allow a whole block of foam to be used if necessary, though usually less is required. The soaked foam is wrapped in the customary polythene and then either impaled onto the poles so that it rests between the two holes before being covered with wire netting, or, if a larger tree is wanted, the foam blocks may be put both sides of the pole and then anchored with the netting. Reel wire is threaded through the holes and through the wire netting, and prevents the foam from slipping.

Use a sharp stick or skewer to make a hole in the polythene for the foliage, and contrive to get a round or triangular outline, for in this case it is appropriate to have geometric trees which look as if they have been recently clipped. The foliage may be put in a day or so before you need the trees, and stout-stemmed flowers added the

One of a pair of matching swags made for a May wedding, to hang in the recesses of the pillars either side of the altar. Hawthorn, cow parsley, 'Bonny Jean' spray chrysanthemums and lime-green Helleborus corsicus, with its large, fat seed pods, look fresh and pretty, especially when the foliage used was mostly the bright Euonymus fortunei 'Silver Queen', with its white variegation. There was also some fluffy Chamaecyparis 'Plumosa'.

The swags were made in similar manner to garlands (see pages 17–18), in 'sausages' of polythene-wrapped, wire netting-encased plastic foam. They were approximately 1.1 metres (3 ft 6 in.) long and it is easy to make them appear longer by giving them trails of ivy at the bottom, or taller top pieces, or both. They will last a long time.

Condition hellebores by just breaking their skin with a pin, from below the flower to the end of the stalk. Then float them in water for a few hours. In the seeding stage they last for weeks. St Giles, Skelton, York. (Arranger: Pauline Mann.)

This small church has a gallery and the two supporting posts were just the right place for the little swags, made to match the windows on page 27 (top) and the pedestal on page 20. They were made using the 'sausage' method with a casing of 2.5 cm (1 in.) wire netting which helps to hold the plant material so efficiently and yet keeps the swag or garland malleable.

Plenty of small-scale, bunchy foliage is wanted for these decorations. These 1 metre (3 feet) long swags contained Euonymus radicans 'Silver Queen', Chamaecyparis pisifera, Viburnum tinus, box and Hedera helix 'Harald', an ivy with an attractive pale variegation. There were also some 'snow' sprayed pine cones, for it was December. Each swag had in it two stems of anemone-flowered and three of spider chrysanthemums and three roses called 'Junior Miss'. Each post had a conveniently positioned painted screw for hanging purposes. St Everilda's, Nether Poppleton, York.(Arranger: Pauline Mann.)

A church porch often has a small window similar to this one where a welcoming arrangement may be placed. This October wedding made use of the last of the 'Iceberg' roses from the garden, along with coral gladioli and spray chrysanthemums. A few deep flame-coloured roses gave an accent and the whole was softened with gypsophila. St Everilda's, Nether Poppleton, York. (Arranger: Pauline Mann.)

One of the window arrangements for a July wedding. The
pew-ends for this wedding
were of pink, white and lilac
sweet peas, so a touch of the
lilac colour was brought into
all the arrangements. The
foliage was Senecio greyii,
Hedera canariensis, peri-
winkle, cotoneaster and ferns.
The flowers were white bridal
gladioli, pink and white
larkspur, erigeron, the modern
border pink 'Show Beauty',
pink spray carnations and the
small pink lily 'Rosario'. All
Saints, Upper Poppleton,
York. (Arranger: Pauline
Mann.)

An example of a sloping
window sill which has had a
wrought-iron platform fixed
to it. The arrangement cleverly
covers the stand. The flowers
were for a December wedding
(see pages 20, 25). The bride
wished for cream and white
flowers that were in season,
but because she was to live
abroad she asked specially for
some roses – roses meant
England to her. The flowers
were the same as those used in
the pedestal and the small
swags were of cream and white
spray chrysanthemums, pink
'Junior Miss' roses and
nerines; the latter were
plentiful and not expensive. A
black, shallow elliptical
container was used and wired
to the wrought-iron stand. St
Everilda's, Nether Poppleton,
York. (Arranger: Janet
Hayton.)

Maximum use was made of the feathery, scented qualities of mimosa in the pew-ends. It has the reputation of lasting no time at all, but the stems used for this early February wedding stayed fluffy and kept their colour for three days before some began to darken and harden. The mimosa was bought in polythene packs, containing special conditioning crystals.

The mechanics were thin laths of wood approximately 18 cm long × 7.5 cm wide (7 × 3 in.) and painted dark green. Small blocks of foam wrapped in polythene or clinging film were capped with a small piece of 2.5 cm (1 in.) wire netting to give support. Reel wire secured the wire netting over the foam through holes drilled through the wood.

Lengths of peg-board, which has ready-made holes, could be used perfectly well instead of wood. All you need is a solid backing to hold the mechanics and lift the wrapped foam away from the wooden pew-ends which might otherwise get stained with water. Finish pew-ends with bows and tails of ribbon if you wish. Each end took three quarters of a pack of mimosa along with Viburnum tinus and juniper. St Olave's, Marygate, York. (Arranger: Evelyn Bough.)

The book markers, made by Mollie Howgate, add interest to an otherwise unadorned piece of church furniture. They were made on wide petersham ribbon and finished with silk tassels. The flowers are silk and they are pretty extras on the scene.

St Giles Church, Skelton, York, decorated with garden flowers for a late July wedding. Larkspur, pink and white foxgloves, catmint, Alchemilla mollis *and* Cornus alba *'Elegantissima' (this needs careful conditioning) have been combined with 'New Dawn', 'Queen Elizabeth' and 'Iceberg' roses.* (Arrangers: Janet Hayton and Pauline Mann.)

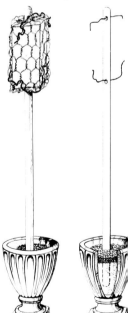

Mechanics for topiary trees.

day before, or early in the morning of the wedding day. Ribbons fixed under the trees to dangle down the poles look pretty, or the poles may have ribbons wound around them; but do wait until the flower and foliage-filled foam have stopped dripping before attaching these – it will only be a short wait.

A tree either side of the church or home doorway will also look good in photographs.

The versatility of the topiary tree is considerable. It can be as small or as large as you choose. Small versions make delightful table decorations, and larger ones look especially well placed either side of steps on a wide, straight staircase. They can also border a length of carpet leading to a marquee. They are striking when used in such a way, and so are garden urns planted with a mixture of ivies and spring bulbs or summer flowers.

The foliage used for these porch decorations was mostly box with the addition of a few wired ivy leaves whose stems were too soft to penetrate the polythene on their own. The trailing pieces were Vinca major.

Viburnum tinus *foliage is to be recommended for topiary trees and garlands; it is very similar to bay and has leaves of just the correct size. It also grows in clusters so that one piece covers a large area. Look for foliage that grows in 'rosettes' at the ends of stems when doing the groundwork on cones, trees and garlands. Choisya ternata is perfect – if you can spare enough. These decorations take more foliage than you expect. Box makes them look very realistic.*

The trees each needed two bunches of spray carnations, (five stems per bunch), two bunches of border pinks (these were in season and obtainable in the market), and three stems of 'Bonny Jean' chrysanthemums. The ball took slightly fewer. You need to choose flowers with strong stems and long-lasting qualities, for although they may be sprayed, they are difficult to water. However, I do often remove the top plant material, open up the polythene and dribble water on to the plastic foam. Do remember to take out the ribbons before you do this in case the trees drip again. You can put them back later. For details of the mechanics of the tree, see pages 24, 30; for instructions on how to make the ball, see page 22. All Saints, Upper Poppleton, York. (Arranger: Elizabeth Duffield.)

A formal triangle on the font, arranged for an early May wedding. There was a mixture of plant material, much of it from the bride's home garden. This included cherry blossom, Spiraea × arguta (bridal wreath), senecio and honeysuckle. The florist's flowers were gypsophila, spray carnations, spray chrysanthemums and Gerbera 'Apple Blossom'. These last blooms were used throughout the church in the other arrangements. St Andrew's, Aldborough, Boroughbridge. (Arranger: Shona Fraser.)

Those who are married during the blossom season are fortunate, for what could be better than a mass of it? This decoration was a mixture of ornamental cherry, pear, and some sprays of the smaller flowered, and brilliantly white, bridal wreath, (Spiraea × arguta) to give a contrast of whites and also to link up with the pew-ends, which were made entirely from the bridal wreath.

The mechanics were two blocks of foam capped with 5 cm (2 in.) wire netting. A board was placed across the uncovered font to hold the shallow tin container. The raised font cover is visible above the blossom.

It is best to cut blossom when the bottom clusters are open and the others in bud. Scrape the stem ends and split them upwards and put them into water for 24 hours. It will last for days. St Olave's, Marygate, York. (Arranger: Pauline Mann.)

An archway for an early spring wedding for a bride who wanted white flowers only. The area of trellis was quite considerable, approximately 8 metres (26 feet) by 50 cm (20 in.), so foliage that had maximum covering ability was needed. Viburnum tinus, Aucuba japonica 'Maculata', Chamaecyparis lawsoniana and berried ivy were available in quantity and gave some variety of form and texture. The choice of flower had to be 'Bonny Jean' chrysanthemums with their beguiling daisy faces, for none of the soft-stemmed spring flowers would have gone into the foam easily enough. Five blocks of well-soaked foam were made into 20 polythene-wrapped packs and wired on to the trellis. Twenty-five stems of chrysanthemums were used. (Archway: Janet Hayton and Pauline Mann; pedestal: Doreen Myers.)

FIVE

THE RECEPTION

Most of the flower arrangements described and photographed in this book are adaptable and so obviously can be used for any occasion as well as for wedding receptions.

THE PRIVATE HOUSE

The area where guests are received is a focal point and a background of flowers is very desirable. In the private house this place is likely to be the hall, if it is big enough. So much may be made of the entrance to a house: topiary trees, floral archways, hanging baskets and balls can be employed in the same manner as described for the church. Inside the home one free-standing arrangement will be enough in a medium-sized hall, and could be too large for a modern house. If the hall is small, think of decorating the banisters and the tops of the door cases or suspending a ball or basket of flowers in the staircase well. Guests will have to pass through the hallway whether they are greeted there or not, and so some flowers are essential.

When the receiving is to take place in a drawing room or other living room a good position is in front of a lavishly decorated chimney piece. This makes an elegant background with the flowers safely out of the way. Try to position all the arrangements high enough to be seen above people's heads, as you did in church; any low groups of flowers will be lost in a room full of standing guests.

Door decorations

Door decorations need not be restricted to wreaths at Christmas time; indeed they do not have to be in the shape of wreaths at all. The one in the illustration on page 39 indicated the room where the wedding reception was taking place. It was made in exactly the same way as a pew-end, with the foam wired to a thin, oblong piece of wood which protected the surface of the door from the mechanics. A handle, knob or knocker is obligatory for fixing it to the door, for it is too heavy for sticky pads. Ribbons and a good luck horseshoe could be added.

HOTELS

Hotels that cater for wedding parties will not usually provide special flower arrangements unless asked to do so. They may well use silk or dried flowers, so make it clear from the start if you want anything out of the ordinary. They frequently have a contract with a florist, or employ someone to look after their plants and flowers. They will not always welcome amateurs or countenance intruders who wish to do the flowers, but they will carry out your wishes and all will be added to the bill.

HIRED HALLS

When a hall is hired for a reception a caterer will need to be chosen and booked too. The caterer usually includes table decorations in the estimate but seldom other flower arrangements, so these must be specially requested. There is no reason at all why you should not do the flowers yourself, or have a friend to do them. Perhaps you could settle the time of your flower arranging with the caterer. It is, after all, for you

A flower arrangement in polythene-wrapped and wire netting-encased foam, wired to the banisters in the bend of the staircase. It can be viewed by everyone and adds an air of festivity to the hall. The time of year was September. (Arranger: Janet Hayton.)

An elegant chimney piece adorned with a Greek key pattern made an excellent background for receiving guests. Trails of Prunus padus, rhododendrons and carnations, lightened with sprays of cow parsley, made up the arrangements for the reception for an early June wedding. The mechanics were taped foam in concealed containers. (Arranger: Beryl Gray.)

Cones of flowers always seem to be in evidence on a special occasion; I suppose this is because a little extra time and trouble has to go into the making of them and this only happens for a celebration. Cones are enormously versatile and can be of any size. They make extremely attractive buffet decorations when they are made taller and slightly wider than those here; these may be placed on old-fashioned cake stands which will give the necessary support. Small versions, about 30 cm (12 in.) high are unusual table decorations for a formal dinner party. For a moderate-sized cone a candlestick and candle-cup are all that is needed. Always choose a candle-cup with a flat base; the curved ones take a great deal of covering.

The pair in the photograph were made for a chimney piece in a room decorated in pale yellow, cream and brown, and used for a wedding reception in the bride's home. The season was late spring. The foliage was Euonymus fortunei 'Emerald 'n Gold', a fluffy chamaecyparis and box. Some Helleborus corsicus added its own lime-green to the 'Emerald 'n Gold'. The flowers were the yellow rose 'Belona', yellow spray carnations 'Tony', a few large matching carnations and pale yellow alstroemerias, all from the florist.

The diameter of the candle-cups was 10 cm (4 in.). These were wired to the candlesticks with reel wire first threaded through the wire netting covering the polythene-wrapped, soaked foam.

Cones and topiary trees can be refreshed by spraying, but they may also have the top pieces of plant material removed, the polythene opened and water carefully dripped onto the foam. Then replace the plant material. Garlands may only be sprayed. (Arranger: Pauline Mann.)

to decide exactly what you want as early as possible and to insist firmly that your wishes are carried out. There is no need to feel diffident or apologetic about something that is of importance to you and for which you will be paying!

MARQUEES

Marquees are so pretty with their fluted linings. The mere sight of one erected on the grass quickens the pulse rate! No scent can compete with that of the crushed grass under the warm canvas. Because the striped linings are so distinctive the flower arrangements need to be bold in colour, otherwise they are likely to be overshadowed. Grey foliage, white, pale pinks, mauves and soft blues are a bit insipid and tend to look washed out alongside the lining colours. The addition of a few vibrant hues will remedy this and a good amount of green foliage provides the necessary outdoor atmosphere as well as giving a definite background that will throw up the colours of the flowers.

Ask for samples of the lining colours when you hire a marquee and choose one that will fit your scheme. The poles will be covered with material matching the lining. The flower arrangers can then make their plans in good time.

Stability of free-standing arrangements
Unless a floor is installed in the marquee the ground will be covered with coconut matting and this is bumpy and uneven. Any pedestals or free-standing arrangements need real care to make them stable. They are best lashed firmly to either the poles or the frame. As in every other crowded situation the flowers need to be well lifted, and decorated poles do this to perfection. The hirers may have chandeliers or some other contrivances to attach to the poles, but if these do not appeal to you there are various ways of fixing the wrapped and wire-covered foam blocks. These are likely to be quite heavy. Stout wire or string may be slotted through the wire

It does not have to be Christmas in order to decorate a door; neither need the style be a wreath. The most important consideration is whether or not there is some sort of knocker or knob on which to hang the flowers. The simple mechanics of a half block of foam, wrapped as usual in polythene and strengthened with 2.5 cm (1 in.) wire netting, held a mixture of grey foliage which included eucalyptus, rue and senecio. The flowers were the annual white lavatera, the silvery peach-pink floribunda rose 'Violet Carson', white sweet peas and gypsophila. Ivy 'Harald' and Thalictrum adiantifolium break up the oval shape. Ribbons and a silver horseshoe would be festive additions. (Arranger: Pauline Mann.)

39

An arrangement on a simple wooden stand with four platforms. It was placed where the bride and groom received the guests and stood on the floor, not on a plinth, so the height was about 2 metres (6 feet). Maximum use has been made of the lovely ornamental crab Malus floribunda, *with its exquisite deep carmine buds that open to pale pink. (The crabs flower later than any of the cherries, so prolonging the season of blossoming fruit trees.) There were two other blossoms in the design:* Spiraea × arguta *and* Prunus *'Kanzan'; the latter has clusters of heavy double flowers. Also included were heads of the bright green bracts of* Helleborus corsicus *which lasts for weeks at this stage of development, and large leaves of the* Arum italicum *'Pictum'. Tulips could have completed the arrangement for there were still some in flower in the gardens in early June, but the rose 'Pink Sensation', with its rich colour and strong stems, was chosen. Twenty roses and nine carnations came from the florist.*

The shallow tins on the platforms had half a block of foam in each, with two blocks in the base tin. They were capped with 5 cm (2 in.) wire netting fixed to the tins with reel wire and also attached to the main stem of the stand with one twist of wire. This prevents the tins slipping if the stand has to be moved. St William's College, York. (Arranger: Pauline Mann.)

Three or five of these 'March stands' would make an eye catching decoration if they were placed along the length of a buffet table. The little 'Mont Blanc' lilies figure prominently amongst the 'Bonny Jean' spray chrysanthemums and late yellow roses. (Arranger: Pauline Mann.)

Plenty of simple countryside materials were used, along with florist's flowers, to decorate the marquee poles. The month was May and the silver birch and beech needed careful conditioning as they were still young and tender. Some Viburnum tinus was also used. The hawthorn was defoliated before it was conditioned. The florist's flowers were pale pink carnations – both large and spray, 'Pink Sensation' roses and gypsophila. Lime-green hellebores and Brussels sprout flowers came from the garden. (Arranger: Catherine Green.)

netting covering the mechanics before it is used to bind them to the posts.

An alternative way is to ask those who put up the marquee to attach ropes round the tops of the poles so that you can tie the blocks to the hanging rope ends. It looks better if moss is placed between the polythene or clinging film and wire netting on the underside of the foam blocks so that the mechanics are hidden – polythene does glint so! The arrangements must be well clear of the tallest heads; avoid long, loose, trailing strands which will catch passers-by and could be pulled out and perhaps spoil your design. Tie these firmly or keep them well out of reach. Arrange the flowers with a picture of a full marquee in mind.

Topiary trees and tubs

Tubs and trees make the best decorations for the approach to the marquee. Cut flowers arranged outside get spoilt by the wind.

SIX

BOUQUETS AND HEADDRESSES

The garland headdress, basket and baskett (a wired novelty design that gives the effect of a basket), are suitable for any age group and are especially appropriate for a summer wedding. The use of ribbons gives movement and adds femininity to the designs.

When making headdresses it is essential to bear in mind the effect which the warmth of the head will have on the flowers; damp cotton wool should be used when wiring to give moisture to the base of the flowers. It is important to have the exact measurement of the head for this particular style of garland.

The delicate headdress was made from white bridal gladioli, gypsophila, cornflowers, spray carnations 'Paradiso', ivy leaves and ribbon. The basket and baskett contained firmly secured foam and the same plant material but with the addition of white freesias 'Miranda', white 'Bonny Jean' spray chrysanthemums and delphiniums. (Arranger: Irene Bough.)

Florists are the experts in the art of creating bouquets and headdresses. This is not flower arranging but wiring, and the florist is trained to choose the correct gauge of wire and to tape it so skilfully that the finished assemblage looks as though it has been lightly and deftly blown together! Florists understand the different conditioning requirements of the flowers they use: whether they will benefit from being sprayed, or have their petals irrevocably marked if this is done injudiciously. They work in cool conditions and have the necessary places where the prepared bouquets, sprays, garlands, wreaths, baskets and balls spend the night before being delivered.

A florist will know what flowers and style of bouquet or posy will suit the dress. He or she will also tactfully take note of the bride's stature and make sure she has the size of arrangement that is in keeping with her height. When a fresh-flower headdress is wanted it is important for the florist to know the hairstyle chosen. A good florist is knowledgeable about design: colour combinations, textures, rhythmic movement, balance and the other elements and principles which, when correctly put into practice, contribute to complete harmony.

There is at present an attractive vogue for having wedding flowers preserved, either by pressing and then reassembling them in a picture, or by drying in a desiccant and making the flowers up under a dome (see page 44). Flowers must be fresh-looking for either of these treatments and must not be marked by

The flowers for the matching bridal headdress and bouquet are available at any time of the year. Internal wiring should be used whenever possible, using gauges light enough to support the plant material. Occasionally two fine wires are better than one of a thicker gauge.

White Dendrobium orchids, 'Mont Blanc' lilies, spray carnation 'Medea', freesia 'Fantasy' and trails of ivy are in both bouquet and headdress.

For assembling these flowers 24-32 gauge wires, florist's tape, ribbon and tissue paper (to cushion the handle of the bouquet) were needed; also a comb to match the bride's hair colour.

The trails of ivy can be rooted (they strike easily) so that the bride may keep a memento of her bouquet. (Arranger: Irene Bough.)

The pink and white roses, mock orange blossom (philadelphus) and lilies of the valley from the bride's Victorian posy were dried in a desiccant (silica gel), and then arranged in the dome. (Arranger: Jean Robinson.)

A Victorian-style posy such as the one shown here is usually carried by a child attendant. Traditionally these attractive posies should have four rings of flowers around a central rose. The fine ribbon loops give movement. Each flower is individually wired and then added. In the centre of the circle is a 'Veronica' rose surrounded by white spray carnations 'White Lily Ann' and 'Silver Pink'. There is also a circle of the pink alstroemeria 'Regina'.

The muff is a design for a winter wedding with the bridesmaids wearing velvet dresses. The same idea could be adapted for a handbag spray or prayer-book decoration. The spray contains red 'Garnet' roses, artificial berries, 'Silver Pink' spray carnations, ivy leaves and asparagus fern.

Also shown here is a ball or pomander for a child attendant. Care must be taken to make sure that the ribbon handle is firmly fixed. Foam or moss may be used as a foundation.

'Carol' roses, gypsophila, pink alstroemeria 'Regina', spray carnations 'Silver Pink' and spray chrysanthemums 'White Hurricane' have been used. (Arranger: Irene Bough.)

wires or water. Tell your florist if you wish the flowers to be preserved. It is very likely that an expert will be recommended to do the job.

There are plenty of books available on the subject of floristry and the amateur can try her hand. It is a fascinating and separate department of flower decoration.

45

SEVEN

CHOOSING THE FLOWERS

Weddings are occasions for enjoying favourite flowers and it is lovely if the church and house can be filled with them, providing they are in season. What could possibly be more memorable than masses of sweet peas or stocks scenting the church, tangles of shrub roses, or the demure simplicity of marguerites and cow parsley?

The triangular outline of an arrangement has become somewhat stereotyped and the mixture of flowers predictable. This is rather sad when there are so many exquisite things to be found, many seldom used. It is a symptom of the economic side of flower growing; certain flowers can be produced all the year round and last a long while when cut – these are the profitable ones. It is often impossible to find simple flowers in the shops, and unless you know a market gardener or grow them yourself you have to do without. It is always worthwhile seeking sources of supply for annuals and border perennials. The market is the place to go to, but if you have an obliging florist he or she may try to get what you ask for.

The ability of a cut flower to live a long time is not an essential virtue for wedding flowers. All flowers are ephemeral and this is part of their wonderful charm. We should be content to capture the beauty of certain blooms just for a day sometimes. This is much easier for country people to do than town dwellers.

The following lists give information as to the availability of various flowers. Whenever possible I have listed plants under their common names, so that they can be more easily recognized by those not familiar with the Latin names of flowers and shrubs. It must be remembered that there are regional differences and that the weather in Britain is temperamental. Flowers which are imported or grown under cover can be relied upon at any time of the year in any part of the country. I have listed these separately. I have ended the chapter with a few thoughts on colour that may be useful in helping with the choice of a colour scheme.

COLOURS

Some colours appear to advance and others to recede; some are warm and others cold; some show well in poor light whilst others vanish. Church buildings are usually on a large scale and tend to be on the sombre side and these factors should be borne in mind.

White and pale colours containing a lot of white are the most visible. Of the pure hues (undiluted colours) yellow, lime-green and orange are easy to see in bad light. Blues, violets and purples vanish in a large building where the lighting is not brilliant. It is said that blue should only be used in churches at mid-summer when daylight strength is at the maximum.

Although white is associated with weddings and white flowers 'show up' better than any others, many brides prefer not to have unrelieved white, although green and white alone are certainly extremely beautiful. When white is used with other colours it should be mixed with soft pastel shades and not with receding or heavy colours. If white is used with receding colours only the white will show at a distance and the flowers will look dotted about.

Name	Description
Alstroemeria (Peruvian lily)	Long stems of irregularly trumpet-shaped flowers borne on pedicles grouped at the top of the stems. A good mixture of colours: cream, peach, salmon, yellow, bronze, red and orange.
Anthurium species	Large, waxy, red, pink and white spathes.
Carnation and spray carnation	Many subtle colours; the only missing hue is blue.
Chincherinchee	Imported flowers with stiff stems of starry white blooms.
Chrysanthemum species	Many species and varieties and an excellent range of colour. No blue.
Fern	Species from all parts of the world, so some are hardy and some tender. Many are delicate and suitable for bouquets.
Freesia species	Very many colours; the only ones missing are a true blue, pink and red. Especially good for bouquets, headdresses and pew-ends. Sweetly scented.
Gerbera species	A daisy-like flower which needs careful conditioning (see page 62). Strong vibrant colours in the orange, flame, yellow, salmon and red band. None with even a hint of blue.
Gladiolus species	Several species including small ones. Long, strong stems. They come in every colour including a mauve-blue.
Heather (shrub)	A large species of evergreen shrubs and sub-shrubs some of which are always in flower. The white heather is thought to bring luck.
Iris (bulbous species)	White, yellow and a strong blue.
Ivy	Evergreen climbing plants, the single leaves of which are commonly wired and used in bouquets. Trails of ivy soften raised arrangements. Indispensable.
Lily	There are so many species, hybrids and varieties that it is possible to obtain some kind of lily at any time of the year, and certain species are available all the year round.
Lily of the Valley	Delicate and sweetly scented flowers, popular for bouquets. They must be one of the least spectacular but most loved flowers.
Orchid	Many species.
Rose	The best-loved English flower.
Stephanotis floribunda	Fragrant, waxy, white flowers.
Strelitzia reginae (bird of paradise)	Strong-stemmed and somewhat rigid in appearance. The flower resembles a crested bird. Overall colour orange.

A garlanded cake for a July wedding reception at Newborough Priory, Coxwold, North Yorkshire. The foliage in the garland was Thalictrum adiantifolium; *the flowers a mixture of garden pinks, alstroemeria,* Achillea ptarmica *'The Pearl', buds of the white rose 'Iceberg' and gypsophila. The mechanics for the garland were a circle of garden hose of a neutral colour split open and packed with soaked foam. These somewhat unusual mechanics did away with any risk of water escaping and dampening the table. The hose would not do for any garland made to hang, for the area for flowers is too restricted.* (Arranger: Eileen Gaskell.)

Shrubs and flowering plants

Name	In the shops	In the garden	Description
Acer platanoides (Norway maple)		April	Bright lime-green flowers appear before the leaves. Will force.
Common alder		Early March	Beautiful catkins.
Allium species	April-May	May-September	Umbels of different sizes and colours. The largest heads of flowers are in the pink to mauve colour range. There are some white and yellow varieties.
Amelanchier canadensis		April	Pure white star-shaped flowers appear before the leaves. Will force.
Amaranthus caudatus (love-lies-bleeding)		June-September	Drooping racemes sometimes as long as 46 cm (18 in.). Splendid in large, raised arrangements. Variety 'Viridis' has pale green flowers.
Antirrhinum species	March-July	June-September	The taller species make good cut flowers. A rich colour range including white, cream, peach and pink.
Artemisia species		May-October	Feathery grey-leaved foliage.
Aruncus species		June-July	Tall, feathery, cream plumes of flowers.
Astilbe species	April-June	June-September	Plume-like heads of small flowers which give a cloudy effect. White, cream and various pinks.
Broom		April-May	Sprays of white, cream, peach, yellow and flame pea-like flowers. Scented.
Buddleia alternifolia		June	Arching branches covered with lavender-blue flowers.
B. davidii 'White Cloud'		July-October	Pure white graceful spikes.
Camellia species	January-February	January-May	Elegant white, pink and rose-red blossoms with beautiful glossy foliage.
Campanula species	May-July	June-September	Bell-shaped white and blue flowers, many varieties, on long stems.
Chrysanthemum maximum (shasta daisy)		June-August	Very many varieties, all white, with single, semi-double, double and frilled petals.

Name	In the shops	In the garden	Description
Clematis species		April-October	*C.armandii* with its white flowers is lovely for an April wedding. *C.flammula* has sweetly scented white flowers borne August-October that last well when cut. Wild clematis (old man's beard) in its seeding form is pretty too.
Cornflower	May-June	June-September	Always thought of as a blue flower although there are pink and white cornflowers. Good as a cut flower and excellent for pew-ends and posies.
Cosmos species		July-September	Pink or white single flowers.
Cotoneaster species		September-December	Curving branches of red berries for autumn weddings.
Cow parsley		May-June	One of the best wild plants for use in flower arranging. Feathery umbels of tiny creamy-white flowers.
Currant, flowering		March-May	When forced in January-February the flowers are white; otherwise they are pink. The shrub has a strong smell which is not liked by everyone.
Dahlia species	July-October	August-October	Many petal shapes and sizes. The colours are vibrant, but there are white and soft hues too. Every shade except blue.
Delphinium species	May-July	June-October	The best tall blue flower. There are also beautiful white varieties. The essence of the English summer. Condition well and with care. Pick when lower flowers are well out.
Eremurus species (fox tail lily)	June-August	June-August	Tall spikes of white, cream, pale peach, pink and yellow star-shaped flowers.
Forsythia species	January-April	February-April	This lovely and plentiful early flowering shrub can easily be forced.
Foxglove		May-August	The common pink or white and the more sophisticated cultivars are good tall, elegant flowers for large designs.

Reception flowers standing on a plinth against a column in the large drawing room at Newborough Priory. The flowers are similar to those in the torchère arrangement on page 17; they were for the same wedding. (Arranger: Eileen Gaskell.)

Name	In the shops	In the garden	Description
Gypsophila species (baby's breath)	June-September and at odd times	June-September	Small fussy white flowers that are extremely softening and pretty, especially for weddings.
Hazel catkins		February-March	A welcome promise of spring and a good addition to arrangements early in the year.
Hyacinth	January-April	March-May	White, blue, cream, yellow, pink and apricot. The single flowers (pips) are wired for wedding bouquets. Very sweet-smelling.
Hydrangea species	April-October	June-October	White, blues, and pinks of many hues. They condition best when mature. They look very well in large mixed arrangements and are especially pleasing in the autumn when the flower heads turn very subtle colours.
Jasminum nudiflorum		December-February	Arching stems bearing small yellow flowers. A lovely winter shrub, much underrated.
Kolkwitzia amablis (beauty bush)		May-June	Flowers resembling small foxgloves are grouped on the twigs. Pink with yellow throats. Extremely pretty and delicate.
Larkspur	June-August	July-August	The annual delphinium which comes in white, various blues and pinks. Often a metre in length. One of the most rewarding annuals and an excellent cut flower.
Lavatera species	July-September	July-September	Pink and white trumpet-shaped flowers.
Lavender	July-September	July-September	Blue, scented spikes for posies.
Lime		July	The flowers are sweet-scented. Strip the leaves and condition the branches with the flowers only.

The simplicity of marguerites used for an early August wedding. An example of decorating both sides of the sill but having one arrangement larger than the other. The trailing foliage was honeysuckle and the big leaves the hostas 'Thomas Hogg' and 'Frances Williams'. All Saints, Upper Poppleton, York. (Arranger: Mattie Young.)

Name	In the shops	In the garden	Description
Lilac	December–April	May–June	One of the best-loved and best-known shrubs. White and mauve to purple panicles. Condition by removing all leaves, splitting the stems and standing in water for at least 24 hours. Use a special sachet (see page 61) in the water. Do not gather when in tight bud.
Lonicera species		June–September	Romantically sweet-scented, and trailing. Not easy to condition.
Lonicera japonica 'Aureoreticulata' (Japanese honeysuckle)		April–November	Small variegated leaves on trailing stems.
Lupin	June	June–August	Familiar summer border flowers with a wide colour range including white and cream.
Mimosa species	December–April		Sweet-scented, small, feathery yellow flowers. Needs careful conditioning with a special sachet of crystals.
Narcissus species	December–May	February–May	Enormous selection; many white varieties.
Nepeta species (catmint)		June–August	Valuable for its delicate grey foliage as well as the small blue flowers. Especially suitable for posies and pew-ends.
Nerine species	October–January	October–December	Shining vivid pink umbels.
Nicotiana species (tobacco flowers)	July–September	July–September	Very sweet-scented. One variety, 'Viridis', is lime-green, and there is also a white.
Paeony	June–July	May–July	Large, satiny, textured flowers, double and single. The single varieties show great golden 'bosses' of stamens. Sweet-scented and very beautiful.
Philadelphus species (mock orange)	June–July	June–August	The perfect white blossom for a wedding. Flowing, sweet-scented branches. Condition carefully, removing nearly all the leaves.

Name	In the shops	In the garden	Description
Phlox species	May-August	June-August	Strongly scented, many-hued heads of bloom including white, soft pink, various mauves and purples and some stronger pinks.
Pyracantha species		September-December	A thorny shrub which bears brilliant shiny orange berries. For the autumn bride who likes such colouring.
Pyrethrum species	May-June	June-July	This herbaceous flower is prolific with its blooms and provides long-stemmed daisies in various tints and tones of pink.
Rose, garden varieties		June-October	Shrub, rambler, floribunda, hybrid tea and climbing varieties all need careful conditioning and some defoliation.
Scabious	May-November	June-September	One of the best soft blue flowers.
Spiraea species		April-May	There are several varieties which have small clusters of white flowers along the length of the branches. One, commonly called bridal wreath (*S. × arguta*) has cascades of blossom and is eminently suitable for a wedding.
Stock	April-August	June-September	Exceptionally sweet-scented and in lovely soft colours of mauve, cream and various pinks; also white.
Sweet pea	April-August	June-September	The perfect flowers for both soft colouring and sweet scent. Ideal for pew-ends and posies.
Sweet william	June-July	June-July	Extremely useful for large mixed arrangements and usually inexpensive and plentiful. The flower heads are pink, red and white.
Symphoricarpos species	September-October	September-December	Graceful curving branches of white berries.
Tulip	January-April	March-May	Every colour except blue. The double, paeony-flowered and lily-flowered types are especially attractive.

55

Name	In the shops	In the garden	Description
Viburnum tinus		Evergreen	A shrub with attractive foliage. It also has pinkish-white flowers from November to March.
Vinca major		Evergreen	Good trailing foliage.
Zinnia elegans	August-October	August-October	Richly colourful blooms, and a green variety, 'Envy'. Stems need a wire pushed up them to keep them straight in arrangements.

Fruit blossom

ORCHARD FRUIT

Name	In the shops	In the garden	Description
Apple		May	Pink in the bud, opening to white. Forces well.
Damson/Plum		April	Usually the earliest fruit blossom. Starry white sprays. Forces well.
Pear		Early May	White blossom. Forces well.

ORNAMENTAL FRUIT

Name	In the shops	In the garden	Description
Malus (crab apple)	May	May	Freely borne white, pink or crimson blossom. Very decorative. Many varieties have attractive fruit in the autumn. Forces well.

PRUNUS

This wide group includes the almonds, peaches, cherries and ornamental plum. They are all beautiful and all will force. I have singled out a few of the best for flower arrangement but they are all desirable.

Almonds:			
P. × amygdalo-persica 'Pollardii'		March-April	Flowers early on completely bare branches. Rich pink flowers.
P. triloba	January-February	March	The easiest variety to come by in florists' shops. Slender straight branches with small pink blossoms.
Cherries:			
P. 'Fudanzakura'		Early	Single pink flowers opening to white. Arching branches.
P. subhirtella 'Autumnalis'		November-March	The winter-flowering cherry. White blossom, whenever the weather is mild. Will force.
Plum:			
P. cerasifera		February-March	Early small white flowers.

EIGHT

PREPARING THE PLANT MATERIAL

The preparation of the flowers and foliage after cutting and before arranging is known as conditioning. It is important that it should be done, for the flowers will then be certain to appear fresh and well groomed. Different flowers need different treatments: the type of stem is usually the guide to this, though there are some exceptions to the general rules. The exceptions are listed later in this chapter.

There are five main stem types: woody, hard, hollow, milky and soft.

WOODY STEMS

Begin by removing any unwanted or damaged leaves from the branches you require for foliage only. When a branch is to be used for its flowers take off nearly all the leaves; a severed branch cannot possibly supply enough water to keep both the leaves and the flowers turgid. The flowers will wilt if the leaves are left on and the removal of the leaves also makes the flowers more visible.

When you have defoliated the branch scrape 5 cm (2 in.) of bark from the cut ends of woody stems before splitting them upwards for 2.5 cm (1 in.). Place the material in deep tepid water and leave overnight, or longer, in a cool dark place.

HARD STEMS

I put roses and chrysanthemums into this group, although shrub roses can also be classed as having woody stems. Remove most of the rose leaves and thorns before splitting the ends of the stems and immersing in tepid water. Chrysanthemums must always have their lower leaves taken off and their stems cut upwards. Treat any other tough-stemmed flowers in the same way, such as paeonies, Michaelmas daisies and phlox. Carnations can have very strong, hard stems; cut these on the slant and always between nodes.

HOLLOW STEMS

Two beautiful well-known herbaceous plants have flowers with hollow stems: the lupin and the delphinium. It helps to prolong their life if these stems are filled with water and then plugged with cotton wool, a piece of crumpled tissue or a bit of plastic foam; these will act as wicks. Lupins 'grow' in water and nothing can be done to stop this happening. They have such lovely colours and seem to me to be such an important part of the English summer border, so it is a shame not to use them. If they are well conditioned and arranged 24 hours before the wedding they can be adjusted a few hours before the event: they will not grow again. Lupins must be well in bloom to condition properly, and delphiniums should have plenty of colour showing in the lower flowers. Remove most of the leaves from both lupins and delphiniums, leaving just a few to give character to the stems.

MILKY STEMS

Some plants exude a milky fluid which is a kind of latex. It will dry at the end of the stem and

A beautifully iced cake on a table draped and decorated with hand-made silk flowers. Silk flowers are so much easier to use in this situation for they do not need water! The flowers were made by Joy Drakeford and the cake iced by Christine Mudge, Bishop Burton College of Agriculture, Beverley.

form a callus which will prevent the uptake of water and cause the flower to die. The way to stop this is to burn the stem end by holding it in a candle or gas flame; alternatively singe it on an electric ring. When the latex stops sizzling it is safe to put the material into water. If the stems are recut the job should be done again. Poppies and euphorbias come into this group. Care should be taken not to come into contact with latex from euphorbias; it may damage the eyes or start a skin irritation.

SOFT STEMS

Often the stems of forced flowers are soft, especially those of tulips and daffodils. When these come from outdoors they are stronger. Always cut off the whitish pithy stem ends from bulb flowers, preferably under water to prevent an air lock, before giving them a drink. Tulips should be wrapped in newspaper before conditioning. This will help to keep them straight. They too 'grow' in water, as do lupins, and may need changing a little in the arrangements just before the wedding. Soft stems can be difficult to get into wet foam and you may need a stick of a similar calibre to make a hole. You can strengthen the stem end by pushing a short length of drinking straw into it. This will allow the flower to continue to take up water for itself.

FIRST AID FOR WILTING FLOWERS

There are often casualties amongst flowers and here are some methods of reviving them if they have wilted. Florist's roses sometimes need attention and I have never known the boiling water treatment fail to restore them. Recut the stem of the flagging rose under water and immediately put it into 2.5 cm (1 in.) of boiling water. Protect the head of the flower with soft paper or cloth. Leave the flower in the water until it cools and by this time it will be as good as new. Wilting, in any flower that has not lived out its expected span, is usually caused by an air lock

and just recutting a stem under water and leaving a flower or foliage to float for a while will revive most flagging materials.

Plenty of flower arrangers burn or boil the stem ends as a routine matter: they are convinced it is the best treatment. Burning or boiling destroys the cells at the bottom of the stem and this prevents micro-organisms surviving to produce slime which will eventually block the water channels and cause an unpleasant smell. Also, because burning and boiling kills the cells, the flower's nutrients cannot escape into the water which can be fouled in this way. Boiling water will also remove an air lock in the stem: this is what often happens to roses.

SPECIAL CONDITIONERS

There have always been tips on how to prolong the life of cut flowers. Some people add a little sugar to the water, or half an aspirin; others may drop a copper coin into the container. It does appear that a few drops of household bleach lengthens the life of certain blooms, especially chrysanthemums and carnations. There are sachets of proprietary brands of crystals made to dissolve in the conditioning water. I have become a great believer in giving florist's roses and carnations this treatment. But, on the whole, use your common sense. Plenty of tepid water and freshly cut stems, dealt with according to their category, work wonders.

FOLIAGE

Mature foliage may be submerged for a couple of hours to good effect. Certainly the large leaves of the hosta and bergenia thrive on being thus soaked. It is possible to make a thin starch solution for large leaves. It is said to keep them stiff in hot weather. Never let grey-leaved foliage go under water or it will lose its greyness.

FLOWERING SHRUBS AND TREES

Any shrub or tree that blossoms before the

leaves come out is easy to condition. Almond, forsythia, *Jasminum nudiflorum*, all the quinces, damson, flowering currant, plum, apple, pear and the delicate bridal wreath or *Spiraea* × *arguta* all present no problems. Later, lilac and philadelphus need nearly all their foliage removing before conditioning, and lilac must be really in bloom before it is gathered or it will die.

SPECIAL NEEDS

✳ Hydrangea heads are composed of flower-like bracts and should be floated for two hours. They condition better and last longer when they are mature.

✳ Euphorbias must all have their stem ends burnt.

✳ Gerberas are best conditioned by being slotted into wire netting suspended over a bucket or tank of water. This not only gives them ample water but also keeps the stems straight. They also respond well to a drink of fizzy lemonade.

✳ Lilies all last well. If you wish to avoid the risk of stained petals and marked clothes remove the anthers carefully: simply cut them off. This does not apply to the arum lily.

✳ Mimosa is now sold with special crystals to be dissolved in the recommended amount of water. Recut the stems, and keeping the mimosa in its polythene bag stand it in the mixture.

LONG-LASTING FLOWERS

Agapanthus species	Lilies, various
Alstroemeria species	Marguerite
Anthurium species	*Nerine* species
Arum lily	Orchid
Chincherinchee	*Protea* species
Chrysanthemum species	*Pyrethrum* species
Clivia species	*Ranunculus* species
Crinum species	*Strelitzia* species
Eremurus species	Sweet william
Heather	

Most daisy-type flowers are long-lasting.

RETARDING FLOWERS

Simple retarding can be brought about by keeping some of the cut flowers in cold water in a cool place and in darkness. It is possible to keep buds in a refrigerator but nothing must be frozen. In the home, soak the stems for two hours and then put the buds into a polythene bag, close the bag and place it low in the refrigerator.

Gladioli and paeonies may be cut a week in advance when the buds begin to show colour. Put them in a cool place, out of water, until two days before they are needed. Then cut 2.5 cm (2 in.) off the stems, under water, before placing in deep tepid water and bringing them into the light.

Rose buds

Rose buds can be kept from opening by having strands of pure wool carefully tied around them. The wool should be removed when the flowers are arranged; they will then open gradually. Another method is to use a little very lightly beaten egg white. With a soft paintbrush touch the inside of the outer petals with the egg white and tie with wool. This glues the petals and they will not unfold when the wool is taken off.

ADVANCING FLOWERS

Branches of spring-flowering trees and shrubs respond best to being forced. The nearer the branches are to their natural blossoming time the quicker they will break into bloom. Those listed below may be cut as soon as the buds show. Scrape the bark from the stem ends and split them for 5 cm (2 in.) before putting them into 5 cm (2 in.) of boiling water for two minutes. Then fill the bucket with tepid water, stand in a warm place and top up with warm water frequently.

The alabaster Madonna and paschal candlestick offered an interesting area for decoration. Towards the end of June those with a generous-sized garden can enjoy the plentiful supply of flowers and foliage. This 1.85 metre (6 foot) group appeared as one whole, but in reality was in two placements. The top container rested on a convenient stone beneath the Madonna, and the lower container was raised on a wooden block approximately 15.25 cm (6 in.) from the ground to allow a downward flow of plant material.

The flowers were the ordinary pink and white foxgloves, Ester Reads, faintly green Aruncus sylvester, Escallonia 'Donard Seedling', Philadelphus 'Belle Etoile' (mock orange), Pyrethrum roseum 'Brenda', a few pink cornflowers and an assortment of paeonies including the familiar double white Paeonia officinalis 'Alba plena'. St Olave's, Marygate, York. (Arranger: Pauline Mann.)

Almond	*Hamamelis* species
Amalanchier canadensis	*Magnolia* species
Apple	*Malus* species
Damson	Pear
Daphne mezereum	Plum
Flowering currant	*Prunus* species
Forsythia species	

WATERING

Flowers drink the most in the first few hours after they have been arranged, so it is important to water the morning after they have been put into place. They may never need as much water again, but if it is crowded and hot they will want attention. Always water and spray with care. Avoid spraying from too close, for some flowers mark easily.

CONCLUSION

In conclusion, I hope this book will help those who are planning a wedding by giving them an idea of where flowers can be placed, and the confidence to go ahead and do them. I have shown seasonal variety and I have deliberately not been extravagant. Obviously more expensive flowers can be chosen if you wish.

Containers are perhaps surprisingly missing from the text and the illustrations, except for pedestals. This is because in a church containers need to be exactly complementary in period, scale, texture and colour to the building. Unless you have the correct urn or vase, a hidden tin is better.

Trouble taken initially in deciding what to have, ordering in good time (with substitute flowers in mind) proper conditioning and assembling the correct mechanics is time very well spent indeed.

May all the brides live happily ever after!

INDEX